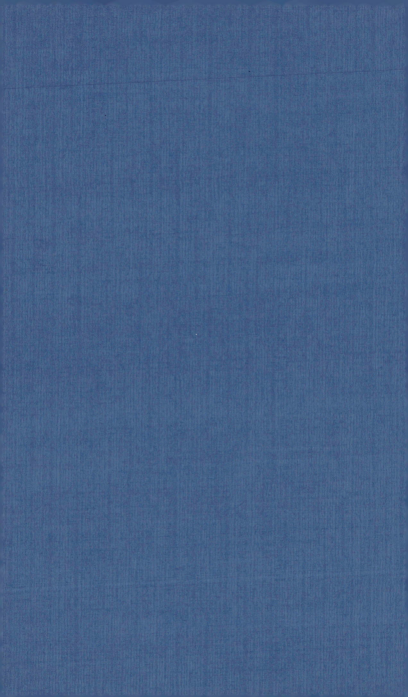

NOW WHAT?

The Chapman Guide to
Marriage After Children

GARY D. CHAPMAN, PH.D.

TYNDALE HOUSE PUBLISHERS, INC.
Carol Stream, Illinois

Visit Tyndale's exciting Web site at www.tyndale.com

TYNDALE and Tyndale's quill logo are registered trademarks of Tyndale House Publishers, Inc.

Now What? The Chapman Guide to Marriage after Children

Designed by Ron Kaufmann

Edited by Kathryn S. Olson

Library of Congress Cataloging-in-Publication Data

Chapman, Gary D., date.
  Now what?: the Chapman guide to marriage after children/Gary D. Chapman.
      p. c.m.
  Includes bibliographical references.
  ISBN-13: 978-1-4143-0017-7 (hc)
  ISBN-10: 1-4143-0017-4 (hc)
  1. Spouses—Religious life. 2. Parents—Religious life. 3. Marriage—Religious aspects—Christianity. 4. Family—Religious aspects—Christianity. I. Title.
BV4596.M3C484 2007
248.8'44—dc22   2007002618

Printed in the United States of America

13   12   11   10   09   08   07
 7   6   5   4   3   2   1

TABLE OF CONTENTS

This is not a book on parenting, though I will share some tips for parents. This is not a treatise on marriage, though I will give some marriage pointers. Rather, this is a book that addresses the question "How do we keep our marriage alive now that the children have arrived?"

This book was born out of a conversation I recently had with a frustrated young father. He said, in a pained voice, "I've lost my wife."

"What do you mean by that?" I inquired.

"I've lost my wife to the baby."

"Tell me about it," I said.

"We've been married for three years and started out with a really good relationship. We both wanted to have a baby and agreed it was time. But if I had known that the baby was going to destroy our marriage, I never would have agreed."

"What do you mean by 'destroy our marriage'?" I asked.

"We just don't have a marriage anymore," he said. "Her life is focused on the baby; my life is focused on the baby. It's like the two of us do not exist anymore. It's like we became parents and lost our marriage."

"How about your sexual relationship?" I asked.

"It's nonexistent. Maybe two or three times since the baby came."

"How old is the baby?" I inquired.

"He turned two last week."

"Have you talked to your wife about your feelings?" I asked.

"I've tried," he said, "but it's hard to talk with her. She says that I don't understand how hard it is to rear a child and work. I told her she could quit work, but she says we can't live on just my salary. I think we could . . . but there's no need to argue with her. I know it sounds selfish, but I just wish I

could have my wife back and it could be like it was before the baby came."

I came away from that conversation knowing I had to write this book. I knew this was not an isolated phenomenon. I've heard similar stories many times during the last thirty years as I have counseled couples about their marriages. I knew also that this young man's wife was as frustrated as he, that she too struggled with the pressures of being both a parent and a spouse. I believe that thousands of couples can identify with this young couple's pain.

In another recent encounter, a young woman approached me with her Bible open. I could tell that she was serious. "When are you going to talk about how children affect a marriage?" she asked.

I had the idea that her question was simply a bridge to something far more personal, so I responded, "Why do you ask?"

"I'm confused," she replied. "It says in the Bible—" she pointed to Psalm 127 "—that 'Sons are a heritage from the LORD. . . . Blessed is the man whose quiver is full of them.' It may be happy

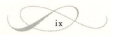

for the man," she said, "but not for the woman. I thought having a baby would pull us together and we would both be happy. The exact opposite is true for us. Since the baby came, our marriage has fallen apart."

I assured her that she was not alone in her frustration, that many couples acknowledge that the first eighteen months after the birth of a child is the most trying time they have ever experienced in their marriage. Mothers of small children often feel isolated and overwhelmed. They feel unwanted or unappreciated by their husbands. They often feel unattractive. "My husband doesn't understand why I am so tired. He complains that I don't bake cherry pies anymore. I'm up to my ears in diapers and vomit, and he's complaining about cherry pies."

Many fathers of young children feel taken for granted by their spouses, unappreciated, and unimportant. They feel that they are no longer number one; the baby has taken their place. They become resentful—not necessarily of the baby, but of the wife's attention to the baby. "She never has time for me. It's always the baby. Even when I ask her to go

out, she's afraid to leave the baby. When I want to rent a video, she says she doesn't have the energy to watch it. I don't know what else to do."

Why is this marital pressure such a common experience? Because a whole new world of potential conflicts arise when a child enters a marriage.

A child means more work. Who does the work? Mom or Dad?

More work means more time. Whose time? Mom's or Dad's?

More work means more energy. Whose energy?

A child means more money. What money—the money that we previously set aside for restaurants and entertainment?

Research has shown that a mother feels the impact of a child upon the marriage most acutely in the first six months of a child's life, when she is trying to adjust to the expanded demands on her time and energy, whereas the father recognizes the impact of the child upon the marriage most acutely during the time the child is six to eighteen months of age. During this time, the husband perceives his wife to be more critical, less supportive, and withdrawing from him sexually.[1]

And unfortunately, the impact of children upon a marriage does not end when the baby is eighteen months old. Jim and Evelyn were in my office seeking help for their fourteen-year-old daughter. After briefly discussing the problems they were having with her at school, they admitted that the main reason they had come to see me was that their marriage was in trouble. "It seems that when it comes to Julie, we disagree on almost everything. Our disagreements on how to rear her have brought us to the point of fighting all the time. Neither of us likes it, but we don't know what to do. It seems we disagree every day on something related to Julie."

I sometimes ask couples, "What was your marriage like before the children came?" I will receive answers like "Well, we were struggling, but we thought a baby would draw us together." Don't expect a baby to create a good marriage; that is not the responsibility of a child. Children do not create a good marriage, nor do they create problems in a marriage; they only reveal problems that were already there. A ten-year study by Carolyn and Philip Cowan revealed that "the most important piece of information to forecast how men and women will fare as parents is how they are doing before they begin their journey to parenthood."[2]

The fact is, rearing children is a joint venture that requires communication, understanding, love, and a willingness to compromise. Couples who have not developed these attitudes and skills before a baby arrives will not find them automatically emerging upon the arrival of the child.

Some couples have good marriages before the children come but five years later realize they have spent so much time being "good parents" that they have let their own relationship grow stale. This kind of staleness does not happen overnight, nor is it the result of open conflict. Rather, it is a slow erosion of intimacy caused by the lack of quality time, expressions of love, and communication. In these marriages, the road to restoration is fairly short because these couples basically have a good relationship that has diminished by default. When one spouse shares

a concern with the other, the two of them will likely make a course correction, and their marriage will get back on track.

On the other hand, for couples who have developed unhealthy patterns of relating before the children came, the road to restoration will be much longer. The changes needed—effective conflict resolution, meaningful communication, tolerance of differences, looking for compromises rather than conquests, and expressions of love in a language one's spouse will feel—require skills that take time to develop. I must add, however, it is never too late to begin. Any couple can learn these skills if they are motivated to do so.

You, too, may be seeking answers to the question, "How do we keep our marriage alive now that the children have arrived?" I believe there are answers to that question, and in this book I will seek to share them.

I have intentionally kept this book brief because I am aware that many couples believe that they don't have time to read a book. You can probably read

this book in less than two hours. And if you do, you will discover how to make time to read books and make time for your marriage. You will also learn how to take control of your finances so that you can accomplish what is of value to you in life. Most important, you will learn how to rekindle marital intimacy and keep it alive while at the same time being good parents. You will find that you are not the only couple who have walked this road. Others have learned how to maintain a healthy marriage while successfully rearing children. You can profit from their discoveries. At the end of each of the five brief chapters, you will find practical suggestions on how to weave these ideas into the fabric of your own marriage.

I assure you that you *can* be happily married and be successful parents at the same time.

1

There comes a time in most marriages when two become three. Sometimes, two become four or five or six or more! This is the design initiated by God in the Garden of Eden when he said to Adam and Eve, "Be fruitful and increase in number; fill the earth and subdue it."[1] Both Scripture and modern sociological research indicate that the best environment for children is the environment created by a loving father and mother who are committed to each other for a lifetime. The Scriptures also indicate that in marriage the husband and wife are to become "one flesh."[2] The term *one flesh* speaks of deep intimacy. Modern research also affirms this concept: Most couples who get married do so because they want to have an intimate, exclusive relationship with each other. If an intimate marriage and parenting are both a part of God's design, then surely there is a way to do both successfully.

Let's freely admit that when children arrive, they greatly affect the marital relationship. There is a new person in the house, and he or she will be there for a long time. That first child may be joined by siblings over the next few years. Each child creates a new dynamic in the household. Someone has said, "The decision to have a child—it's momentous. It is to decide forever to have your heart go walking around outside your body."[3] Parents can identify with that statement. The child is a part of them, and their hearts are linked to the child's well-being. However, in their love for the child, they must never forget that the child is the offspring of their love for each other. Therefore, they must continue to cultivate that love relationship, not only for their own well-being but for the well-being of the child as well.

When a couple neglect their own love relationship, either intentionally or unintentionally, they

do so to the detriment of their children. Research clearly shows that the effect of divorce upon a child is devastating. Divorces typically do not occur on the spur of the moment. They are preceded by months and sometimes years of neglecting the marital relationship. Therefore, for the conscientious parent, there is nothing more important than rekindling or keeping alive an intimate relationship with his or her spouse. The antidote to divorce is to stop the process of drifting apart. Choose to paddle your canoes toward each other rather than away from each other. In the last chapter of this book, I will tell you how to do that. But first you must commit yourselves to the process by *making marriage a priority*.

What does it mean to make marriage a priority? It means, first, that we pause long enough to assess the quality of our marriage. Then we must make a conscious choice that, for the benefit of our children, for ourselves, and (if we are Christians) for the glory of God, we will commit ourselves to each other and acknowledge that our marriage is important to us. Finally, we must agree that with

God's help we will find a way to strengthen our intimacy. Making marriage a priority is a conscious choice to make things better.

There is a song that says, "Love and marriage go together like a horse and carriage."[4] I would like to change part of that analogy and say that *marriage and parenting* go together like a horse and carriage. The horse and the carriage exist as separate entities; they can be separated from each other. When the horse is separated from the carriage, it is free to roam and frolic as it likes. In a similar manner, marriage and parenting are separate endeavors, but parenting is at its best only when it is linked with marriage.

When the horse is harnessed to the carriage, its freedom is limited, but its energy can be used for positive purposes. The carriage cannot fulfill its created function without the horse. Before children, a husband and wife are able to roam and frolic as they choose. Once children come, parents' freedom is limited. But their choice to be connected with their children is for the good of both parents and the children.

However, limited freedom does not equal no freedom. The horse is often uncoupled from the carriage and returns to the pasture—a horse that stayed harnessed to the carriage day and night would soon become a frustrated horse. Nor would this be good for the carriage and its passengers. Similarly, a couple who are so attached to their child or children that they have no time for themselves will become a frustrated couple. This is not good for the children or the parents.

Like the horse apart from its carriage, parents have an existence apart from their children. This existence is called marriage, which at its best provides parents time to frolic and enjoy each other so that they are renewed for their task of parenting.

Please note that the title of this chapter is "Making Marriage a Priority." Notice I say *a* priority. I often encounter couples who argue over whether the child should be their priority or marriage should be their priority. That's like arguing over whether water or food should be *the* priority for the human body. The truth is they are both priorities. Parents who do not seek to be good parents are delinquent in their responsibilities. On the other hand, couples who do not give priority to their marriage are also delinquent.

A couple who neglect their children in pursuit of their own happiness will live to regret their decision. On the other hand, a couple who neglect their marriage while focusing all their energy on their children will also live to regret their choice.

Keeping your marriage vibrant and alive is one of the best things you can do for the health of your children, who will also likely one day be married. They desperately need a model of what a healthy marriage looks like. If you neglect your marital relationship, you may meet the children's physical needs but realize in time that you have failed to teach them relational skills. Marriage is a priority; parenting is a priority—the choice is not either/or. To neglect either is detrimental to the other.

In my book *The Four Seasons of Marriage,*[5] I used the seasons to describe the various stages of a marriage:

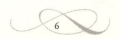

- **Springtime** in marriage is a time of new beginnings, new patterns of life, new ways of listening, and new ways of loving. Feelings we experience during this season include excitement, love, trust, hope, and joy.

- **Summer** couples share deep commitment, satisfaction, and security in each other's love. They are connected and supportive of each other.

- **Fall** brings a sense of unwanted change, and nagging emptiness appears. We might feel apprehensive, concerned, sad, discouraged, and uncertain.

- **Winter** means difficulty. Marriage is harder in this season of cold silence and bitter winds. Couples experiencing a winter season in their marriage will act and feel harsh, angry, disappointed, and detached.

You may want to ask, "What season was our marriage in before the children came? What season is our

marriage in now?" If you are not happy with your present season, *Now What?* is definitely for you. In the next four chapters, I will share practical ways of restoring and maintaining a healthy marriage while at the same time being successful parents.

PUTTING THE PRINCIPLES INTO PRACTICE

1. Using the idea of the four seasons, assess the quality of your marriage by underlining the words in each description that best describe your current feelings about your marriage. Then ask your spouse to read this chapter and make an assessment as well.

2. If you discover that your marriage is in the unsettledness of fall or the coldness of winter, you need not remain there. You and your spouse can return to the spring or summer seasons of marriage by confessing your failures to each other and asking forgiveness.

3. Can you both agree to make your marriage a priority? Your motivation may be for the

children, for yourselves, or for God. But whatever your motivation, when you make marriage a priority, you are moving in the right direction.

2

TAKING CONTROL OF YOUR SCHEDULES

$\mathcal{I}$n my experience, the issues that are most likely to lead to conflict between a husband and wife in any stage of parenting are the division of the workload in the family, the amount of time spent together as a couple, frustration about their sexual relationship, management of family money, the need for time alone, differing ideas about rearing children, communication with each other, and a willingness to work on improving their relationship. It's obvious that processing all these issues will take time. But where does this time come from? We already sense that there is not enough time available to do what needs to be done. I believe that the answer to finding time to build a strong marriage, while at the same time being good parents, lies in *taking control of our schedules.*

Taking control of our schedules means that we consciously examine who is doing what and when it is being done, looking for a better solution. Marital schedules involve two factors: Who will do what? and When will it be done? Many couples have never thought seriously about their marital schedules. They have simply drifted into a pattern of operation largely dictated by what they saw their parents do. This pattern may be effective or ineffective. If their marriage is suffering, their pattern is likely highly ineffective.

GET THE RIGHT PERSON DOING THE RIGHT JOB

In family life, certain tasks must be done, and done regularly—some daily and some weekly. The first step in getting control of your schedule is to make a list of these daily and weekly tasks. Once the list is made, the two of you can evaluate which of you is best equipped to do each task. (When children are small, there are only two people to do these tasks: the husband and the wife. As the children grow, they can be brought into the work team and learn experientially what it means to be a member of the family.)

The key is getting the right person doing the right thing so that both partners are maximizing their abilities for the benefit of the team. For example, he may be a great cook but is not adept in operating a lawn mower, whereas she may find mowing the lawn relaxing and even enjoyable. If he has been mowing the grass for the first three years of their marriage (because his father did), and she has been cooking during those years (because women are "supposed" to do the cooking), they have both likely found their tasks burdensome and drudgery. However, if they shift their responsibilities, letting him do what he enjoys most and letting her do what she enjoys most, they can intensify their emotional energy and their sense of well-being.

DECIDE WHEN TASKS WILL BE DONE

Once they have agreed on who will do what, based on their interests and abilities, the second step is

to decide when they will do these tasks. Again this requires teamwork. While she is mowing the grass, he agrees to stay inside and take care of the children. If the children are young, perhaps he can balance the checkbook and pay the monthly bills while keeping an eye on the children. If they are older, he may be helping them with homework or playing with them. If his vocational commitment makes this impossible, then perhaps they could afford to pay a sitter to watch the children while she mows the grass. If finances are limited, perhaps she could work out an exchange program with a friend where they agree to keep each other's children for a few hours while the other completes a task. If he is going to cook the evening meal three nights a week, it may require her helping the children with homework while he does his task. If his work schedule gets him home later, then dinner may have to be later on those evenings.

ELIMINATE UNNECESSARY TASKS

Taking control of our schedules also involves asking the question, "What are we doing or trying to do that may not be necessary?" I remember the wife who was frustrated because, before the baby came, she dusted the house every other day (because her mother had done so). After the baby came, she found this to be extremely stressful. When she was not able to accomplish the task, she felt she was failing in her responsibilities. Once we examined the issue, we discovered that her mother dusted every other day because she lived on a dirt road and kept the windows open during the summer. The daughter's house was on a paved street, and it had air-conditioning. What made sense for her mother made little sense for her. Upon discussing it with her husband, they both agreed that dusting once a week was acceptable to both of them. Eliminating unnecessary tasks creates time that can be set aside for marital enrichment.

I remember the husband whose wife complained about his playing golf every Saturday. His viewpoint was, "This is my only day for relaxation. I find golf relaxing." As we examined the situation, we discovered that his father had played golf every Saturday and had taught his son to do the same thing. Her complaint was that on Saturday there were household tasks that needed to be done, since both of them worked during the week. So on Saturdays, she worked while he played. Then he came home and wanted to have sex. She resented this arrangement.

It took a few counseling sessions, but eventually the husband discovered that he much preferred sex over golf. He started spending Saturday mornings doing some of the weekly tasks with his wife. In the afternoon they sent the children to the YMCA for swimming lessons, and every Saturday, they experienced an afternoon delight. Getting control of our schedules may mean that we cannot continue doing all the things we have been doing.

GET YOUR CHILDREN ON A SCHEDULE

Schedule control also involves getting your children on a routine that interfaces positively with your schedule. You are not stifling their creativity when you help children establish scheduled living. Children actually thrive best when their lives have boundaries. A child who grows up without boundaries will be an undisciplined teenager and an irresponsible adult.

Establishing consistent times to go to bed and to get up in the morning is a good place to start setting boundaries for your children. I am always amazed when I see four-year-olds in the local Wal-Mart at 10 p.m. Little wonder that parents complain they don't have time for each other. Four-year-olds should be in bed long before ten o'clock. Then Mom and Dad will have time for some of the important things we've been discussing. They might read and discuss a book on marriage in order to learn to communicate with each other positively. They can learn to respect each other's ideas and find resolutions to their differences. And they will have time to enjoy sexual intimacy.

You must decide what you think is realistic, but I suggest a bedtime of seven o'clock for children up to the age of eight. After that, you might begin to extend their bedtime, but never more than fifteen minutes per year. That means that at age twelve, a child's bedtime would be eight o'clock. Whatever you decide, remember that a consistent bedtime for the children is good for them and for your marriage.

It is not just bedtimes that need to be scheduled. Children need a schedule for the day as well. During the preschool years, there should be a time for art; a time for listening to parents read a book to them; a time to help parents with cooking, setting the table, sweeping, and folding the clothes; and a daily period of time in which the child is alone in his or her room playing with toys and learning to be creative. There should also be regular nap times. Children should not be forced to go to sleep, but simply to lie down and rest. If they sleep, fine; if they don't sleep, fine—but everybody takes a daily rest. It is the room times and the rest times that give parents time to read books, to rest, or to do anything that they find meaningful. As the children get older, there is also time scheduled for homework and chores. Putting your children on a schedule is not only good for the children but enhances your own physical, emotional, and spiritual well-being.

If you have parents who live nearby and they want to be involved in the lives of your children, this also should be scheduled. When relatives pop in whenever and wherever, their presence can be annoying because it interrupts your planned program for the afternoon or evening. But when you schedule time for your children to be with their grandparents, then it allows you and your spouse to do something that enhances your marriage.

MAKE TIME FOR YOURSELF

Scheduling also provides time for each of you to be alone. All of us need some time apart from the pressures of family life. Spending time alone is not selfish. No one can be "on duty" twenty-four hours a day for an extended period of time without becoming emotionally and physically depleted. This is never good for a marriage. You need time alone to breathe deeply, enjoy the beauty of nature, and commune with God. This time should be spent in doing something that you find invigorating or relaxing. It can be playing golf, reading a book, watching television, taking a walk, or working out at the local gym—anything that invigorates your mind or your spirit. Organizing everybody's schedules in such a way that each of you can have time alone is an essential ingredient to building your marriage.

In summary, getting control of your schedule means getting the right person doing the right task and deciding when it will be done, eliminating any unnecessary tasks that you are presently doing, getting your children on a schedule that interfaces positively with your schedule, and making time for yourself.

All this will help enable the two of you to engage in marital enrichment times in which you can learn to process your differences and give loving support to each other, thus building intimacy.

PUTTING THE PRINCIPLES INTO PRACTICE

1. Make a list of all the tasks that must be done regularly (either daily or weekly). Ask your spouse to make a similar list. Then bring your two lists together and make a composite list. Now each of you take a copy of the comprehensive list of tasks and put your initials by the ones you think you are best equipped to do or would most enjoy. If there is something you think the two of you should share, then

put both of your initials, but underline the
person you think should take the basic
responsibility for that task. Then come
together and discuss your lists. See where you
have agreed and where you have disagreed.
Where you disagree, negotiate. You need not
keep these assignments forever, but for the
next few weeks, try this plan. You may find
that getting the right person doing the right
task will radically change your perspective on
household chores.

2. Agree on the day of the week and/or the
approximate time each day that each task
will be performed. For example, if the
husband is going to take the responsibility
for taking the garbage outside, will he do this
at the end of each day or at the beginning of
each day? Getting on the same page can
eliminate a lot of tension between the two of
you. Knowing that he is going to cook the
evening meal on Tuesday and Thursday can
help both of you plan your schedules in a
supportive manner.

3. What is the first step you need to take in getting the lives of your children scheduled? If your children are older, expect some opposition. But once they see that you are kind but firm, they will "get with the program."

4. What changes would you like to see in your time alone? What steps will you take to make these changes?

5. If you had more time to be with your spouse, what would you like to do? Compare your answer with your spouse's answer, and negotiate a way to make it happen.

3

TAKING CONTROL OF YOUR MONEY

*T*hey were in my office. She was weeping uncontrollably. He was outwardly stoic, but I could tell he was deeply frustrated. Seven years and two children into their marriage, it was in shambles.

From her perspective, before they were married, he was romantic, loving, and caring. After the wedding, he became cold, withdrawn, and self-centered. With tears flowing freely, she said, "All I've ever wanted is a husband who will love me, who enjoys being with me—someone with whom I can share life. Is that too much to ask? I thought we had this before we got married. I don't know

GARY CHAPMAN

what happened, but after the wedding, he was like a different man. Two years later, we had our first child. I thought that would bring us together, but I was wrong. Then came the second child. He started helping more around the house, but there was never any time for us. I felt like we were roommates taking care of two children. I love my children, but I also want a husband who will talk with me. I want us to have a life apart from raising children."

When I looked at her husband, he said, "I'm sorry I haven't been able to meet her needs. Finances have been tight. I have a good job, but I'm not a rich man. She works only part time. She likes gifts; she wants to go places and do things. All of that costs money, money that we don't have. I've been trying to save money so we can buy a house. I know that she doesn't like where we are living. There's just not enough money to do everything."

Later, when we looked at their financial situation, we discovered that they were an average family with an average income. The problem was they had never integrated their marriage and their money. He had been saving every penny to make a down payment on a house. In addition to his full-time job, he had worked a part-time job three evenings a week, and every extra dollar had gone into the housing fund. While she, too, wanted to buy a house, she would have preferred an intimate marriage. When he was at home, he spent time with the children and time watching sports events on television, but little or no time with his wife. Consequently, she was at a point of desperation. They were now living in their new house, and they were miserable. Upon reflection, he also agreed that the marriage was more important than the house, but this had not been reflected in his actions.

PUT YOUR MONEY WHERE YOUR PRIORITIES ARE

There is a simple principle that, when applied, will keep a marriage alive regardless of a couple's income. The principle is this: Put your money where your priorities are. If the marriage relationship is a priority—and if special gifts, a weekly date night, and occasional weekend getaways will enhance the marriage—then invest money in making these a reality. The house may come two or three years later than anticipated, but at least you will have a marriage to place in the house. The house will be a home rather than a boarding place.

Without question, children are expensive. One recent report indicated that to rear a child from birth to college will cost approximately $250,000.[1] To the average couple, such figures may seem overwhelming. The good news is that, especially in the United States, the opportunities for successfully financing a family are unlimited. There are numerous ways to cut corners, save, and invest that make it possible to have a successful marriage and rear healthy children on almost any level of income. The key is in utilizing these opportunities. Far too often couples get caught up in mimicking their neighbors' lifestyle rather than thinking creatively about how to accomplish their own priorities.

If our priorities are a healthy marriage and creating a positive learning environment for our children, then our money should be channeled toward reaching these objectives rather than following the materialistic lifestyle of our neighbors. If you are feeling that you do not have enough financial resources to do the things that enrich your marriage, then it is time for you to *take control of your money.*

There are only two basic methods to increase funds to invest in your marriage. They are simple to state but require effort to implement. One is lowering your expenditures, and the other is increasing your income. In my opinion, the easiest place to start is in lowering your expenses. In the next few paragraphs, there are some practical suggestions for doing this. Some of these will require a change of attitude, but it will be a change that will greatly enhance your marriage relationship.

SPENDING LESS AND ENJOYING IT MORE

There are numerous ways to increase a couple's marital-enrichment fund by spending less. Bob and Jean live in southern Illinois. At one of my marriage seminars, they shared with me that they had saved thousands of dollars by *recycle shopping*. It all started with an experiment. They agreed that for six months they would buy all their household items, all their clothes, and all the children's toys and school supplies at one of three places—the local Goodwill store, Salvation Army store, or consignment shop. After six months, they were hooked.

"We love it," said Jean. "The things we buy are high quality, and we get them at really good prices."

Another couple who live in Florida told me they had found something even better than shopping at Goodwill. "We call it *free shopping*," the husband said.

"How does that work?" I asked.

"Three things," he said. "First, we drive through affluent neighborhoods the night before the discards are to be collected. It's amazing the things you find sitting beside a garbage can. Recently, we found a perfectly good basketball goal. We brought it home, and our kids love it. At first, we felt guilty that maybe we were stealing. So now, we ring the doorbell and ask the family if they would mind our having whatever is sitting beside their garbage can. We've never had anyone refuse to give it to us.

"The second approach is that we have let all our friends know we are open to receiving hand-me-downs, especially children's clothing and toys. We get more than we need, so we pass what we can't use along to others.

"The third approach is to inform our parents of specific toys that our children have requested. We know that they are going to give the children presents for birthdays, Christmas, and other occasions, so why not have them purchase things that the children really want?

"With these three approaches, about the only thing we have to buy our children is food. And now that the children are older, next summer we are going to start a garden," he said with a smile.

Another way to save money by spending less is *seasonal shopping*. My wife is an expert in this kind of shopping, which is especially helpful when buying clothing. Karolyn likes to wear nice clothes, and I like to see her in nice clothes. But she never pays full price for anything. She always shops at the end-of-season sales. I don't mean the

first day of the sale; I mean after items have been reduced one, two, or three times. The other day she came home with a $399 outfit that she had bought for $59. I love the woman, and I love her skills. I told her, "We could not afford for you to work outside the home because you wouldn't have time to save us all this money." Actually, the money she saves by seasonal shopping provides a rather good "income."

When it comes to food and household items, there is also *discount shopping*. In most towns, there is a good store that sells cheaper than all the rest. Why not buy your groceries there? Their bananas came off the same boat as the bananas at the more expensive store. And by using manufacturer's coupons, you can save even more. Buying at the cheapest store, using coupons, and stocking up on the special-sale items can save literally hundreds of dollars in your food and household budget.

With all these additional funds, you can pay for that weekend getaway, start a savings fund for your children's college education, and save money for the new house. These savings can be channeled toward your priorities—an enriched marriage and healthy, responsible children.

INCREASING YOUR INCOME

The second basic method of having more money for your marital-enrichment fund and family-fun fund is to increase your income. One way to do this is by saving and investing. Typically, a savings account is established to accomplish a particular objective such as taking a family vacation, buying a new car, or preparing for your child's education. On the other hand, investing involves putting discretionary funds to work for you. The yield on investments is usually higher over the long haul than the yield on savings accounts. But realize also that there are greater risks with investing. Never invest money that you really need for something else. Invest only money that you could afford to lose. Many couples have failed to follow this principle and have created severe financial pressure.

A second way to increase your income is for one of you to take on additional work. This may be a part-time job in the home or outside the home. Two guidelines should be followed when exploring this possibility: First, make sure that you understand the requirements of the job before you take the plunge. Second, assess with your spouse the impact this additional job will have on your marriage relationship. Remember, your ultimate priority is a better marriage, not more income. If the income will enhance your marriage and the job will not detract from your intimacy, then perhaps it is a good move.

Let me conclude this chapter by saying that the best things in life are free—or at least inexpensive. Taking time to enjoy a sunset, picking a wildflower and giving it to your spouse, enjoying the colors of fall leaves, going to church, taking a walk together, or sitting together on the porch while the crickets serenade you costs nothing! Sharing icecream cones, eating your favorite pizza, taking a swim, or attending a movie together are all relatively inexpensive.

The challenge of this chapter is for you to take control of your money so that you will have the necessary funds to enrich your marriage on a regular basis as well as provide for the material needs of your family.

PUTTING THE PRINCIPLES INTO PRACTICE

1. At the present time, is the way you handle finances working *for* your marriage or *against* your marriage? Is decreasing your expenditures to increase funds for enriching your marriage an option you are willing to consider? If so, which of the following seem to be most feasible to you?

   Recycle shopping
   Free shopping
   Seasonal shopping
   Discount shopping

2. Discuss these with your spouse and agree on a spending plan for the next six months.

3. Are you pleased with your present pattern of saving and investing? If not, what would you like to change? Discuss these changes with

your spouse and see if you can agree on a
more productive plan.

4. Is there a realistic possibility that one of you
could accept additional work for the purpose
of producing additional income? How would
this impact your marriage relationship?
Explore this possibility with your spouse.

4

$\mathcal{O}$ne of the most common areas of conflict between husbands and wives is how to discipline the
children. "He's too harsh," the wife says. "She lets
them get away with murder," the husband responds.
The conversation goes downhill from there, each
accusing the other of being too lenient or too hard
on the children. When a couple are continually
having these kinds of arguments, it obviously has
a detrimental effect on their marital relationship.
Each parent has a genuine concern for the well-
being of the children. However, their arguments
leave them wounded and resentful.

If that sounds familiar, this chapter will help you and your spouse get on the same page with regard to effective discipline. The word *discipline* is not a negative word, nor is it to be equated with spanking or yelling at children. The word *discipline* means literally "to train." Most parents recognize that children need training. Without positive discipline, children will self-destruct; they cannot train themselves.

The problem is that most parents have had little or no instruction in how to effectively train children. Therefore, they come to parenting with only the example of their own parents. If they perceive their parents as good parents, they will try to follow those models. If they perceive their parents as poor parents, they will try to do the opposite.

At any rate, their views of proper discipline will often bring them into conflict. For the sake of their marriage, they desperately need to get on the same page. For the sake of their child, they need to make sure they are on the *right* page. Children are greatly influenced by their parents. We want to make sure that the influence is positive.

To be good parents, we must understand the fundamentals of rearing children. The basics of child rearing are not difficult to understand, although they require the willingness to change negative patterns and consistently establish positive patterns.

CHILDREN NEED TO FEEL LOVED

The first fundamental in rearing children is that children need to feel loved by their mother and father. Children who do not feel loved and respected by their parents will grow up with many emotional struggles, and their behavior will reflect these emotional struggles. Most parents sincerely love their children, but thousands of children do not feel loved. The problem is that parents are not communicating love in a language that children can understand.

In my research, I have discovered there are five fundamental ways of expressing love. I call them the five love languages. Let me share them briefly.

The first is Words of Affirmation—using words to communicate to a child how much you love him or her, expressing appreciation to the child when he/she does something worthy of commendation, and using words of encouragement when the child is fearful. Here are examples of Words of Affirmation: "I love you sooo much." "I like your art. The way you blended the colors together makes it look exciting." "Thanks for helping Mommy set the table." "I appreciate your taking the trash outside for me." "I think you can make the team because you have a lot of drive, but you will never know until you try. If you really want to do it, I would encourage you to try. If you don't make it, you can try again next year."

The second love language is Acts of Service— doing something for your children that you know they would like for you to do: mending a doll's dress, repairing a bicycle, pumping up a football, baking their favorite cake, or teaching them to swim. All these are acts of service. The emphasis is on doing things for your children that they cannot yet do for themselves. Later, you serve them by teaching them how to pump up footballs and repair bicycles.

The third love language is Gifts. The giving and receiving of gifts is a universal expression of love. I would be quick to emphasize that the gifts need not be expensive and that we need not give our children everything they desire. To do so would be poor parenting indeed. But if gifts express love, then even simple gifts like stones you pick up from a public parking lot or a flower from the yard will communicate that they are loved.

The fourth love language is Quality Time—giving your child your undivided attention. Perhaps you are playing a game or reading a book; perhaps you are having a conversation. The important thing is that the child has your attention. You are not watching television, talking on the telephone, or fiddling with a pencil. Your child has your undivided attention.

And love language number five is Physical Touch—hugs and kisses, pats on the back, friendly wrestling on the floor. All these communicate love.

Out of the five love languages, each child has a primary love language. If you want your child to feel loved, you must give heavy doses of his or her primary love language while sprinkling in the other four as icing on the cake. If you don't speak a child's primary love language, the child may not feel loved even though you are speaking some of the other languages. This simple insight has helped thousands of parents learn to express love to their children effectively.[1]

CHILDREN NEED TO KNOW THERE ARE RULES

A second fundamental in child rearing is to understand that there are rules. There are some things we do and some things we don't do. All societies are built on a concept of dos and don'ts. Without such rules, society could not exist. Children must learn this reality. This requires parents to decide together about the rules they intend to teach their children. Healthy rules are always reasonable. They serve some positive function. Therefore, parents need to ask themselves whether a rule is good for their child and whether it will have some positive effect on their child's life. Here are some practical questions that will help you evaluate rules:

- Does this rule keep a child from danger or destruction?

- Does this rule teach the child some positive character trait: honesty, hard work, kindness, sharing, etc.?

- Does this rule protect property?

- Does this rule teach the child to take care of his/her possessions?

- Does this rule teach the child responsibility?

- Does this rule teach good manners?

Answering questions like these will help you come up with healthy rules for your family. These are the factors about which we are concerned as parents. We want to protect our children from danger and destruction. We do not want our young children to be hit by a car in the street. And we do not want our older children to get involved in drugs. We want to teach our children positive character traits in keeping with our values. We want children to respect the property of others, so a rule about not playing baseball in the backyard may keep them from breaking the neighbor's window. We want them to learn to take care of their own possessions; therefore, a rule about putting their bicycle in the storage shed at night is a purposeful rule. We want our children to respect others, so we teach our children to look adults in the face and say yes, sir and thank you.

We want our children to be responsible adults, and we know that they must learn this in childhood. Therefore, requiring a child to be responsible for making his bed or vacuuming her floor is a reasonable rule. And what of good manners? It is interesting that contemporary corporate executives are hiring etiquette trainers and consultants because instead of social graces, contemporary employees are characterized by rudeness and crudeness. I believe this can be traced to the lack of teaching manners in the home. If as parents we believe that "please" and "thank you" are better than "gimme" and "yuck," then we will have rules regarding such manners in the home. Other parents, teachers, extended family, books, and magazine articles are perfectly legitimate resources in making family rules. To have the best possible rules, parents need all the knowledge and wisdom they can get.

Once parents agree on the rules, two issues become extremely important: First, *the rules must be clearly explained to the children.* Parents often assume that children automatically know what they are to do or not to do. This is not the case. We must clearly express our expectations to children. The entire family needs to be aware of the rules. Unspoken rules are unfair rules. A child cannot be expected to live up to a standard of which he or she is unaware. Parents have the responsibility for making sure that children understand what the rules are. As children grow older, they also need to know *why* their parents have decided on these rules. If children feel genuinely loved by their parents, they will usually acknowledge and value such rules.

The second important issue with regard to rules is that once the rules are made, *the consequences for breaking the rules also need to be established.* Obedience is learned by suffering the consequences of disobedience. Effective teaching of obedience requires that consequences for breaking rules should cause discomfort to the rule breaker. It is especially helpful if the consequences for breaking family rules can be determined and discussed with the family at the time a rule is made. This has the advantage that the child knows ahead of time what the consequences of breaking a rule will be, and it delivers the parent from the peril of having to make a snap judgment about what discipline should be applied. Deciding the consequences before a child breaks a rule is also more likely to establish a reasonable consequence.

If a rule is that we don't throw a football inside the house, what are the consequences if that rule is broken? A logical consequence might be that the football is put in the trunk of the car for two days and that the child must pay from his or her allowance for anything that was broken when the football was thrown. Mr. Jones's window, broken by a baseball hit from the backyard, should require a verbal apology to Mr. Jones and payment for the window repair out of Johnny's hard-earned money. Such consequences will likely motivate Johnny to play ball in the park and not in the yard.

If a rule is that your children do not smoke cigarettes, then if your son is caught smoking, he must immediately eat a carrot—the whole thing.

This will give the body beta-carotene to overcome the nicotine, and chances are he will think twice about smoking another cigarette. If there is a second violation, having him make a $25 donation to the American Lung Association, pick up one hundred cigarette butts from the street, and read an article on the dangers of nicotine to the lungs will probably be enough to convince him that smoking is not for children.

From these illustrations, perhaps you see the emerging pattern that consequences should be as closely associated to the rule as possible.

I am often asked, "What about spanking as a consequence for disobedience?" In my opinion, it is usually far more effective to tie the consequences to the behavior. For example, in the illustration given above about Johnny's breaking the window because he broke the rule about playing baseball in the backyard, facing Mr. Jones next door and paying for the window are far more meaningful than giving Johnny some swats for disobedience. Spanking a child is not a cure for all misbehavior. In fact, it may be a reflection of a parent's unwillingness to invest time trying to teach the child obedience.

COMBINING DISCIPLINE WITH LOVE

When a rule is broken and the parent is required to make sure that the child experiences the agreed-upon consequence, it is extremely helpful to give your child a dose of emotional love before and after the discipline. It is most helpful when you use the child's primary love language.

For example, let's say that your son was playing football in the living room, a clear violation of rules. Let's say that the child's primary love language is Words of Affirmation. The parent might say something like this: "I think you know that I love you very much. Normally, you follow the rules quite well. I am proud of you and your many accomplishments at school and at home. You make me a very happy parent. But when you break the rules, you know that you must suffer the consequences. So, let's put the ball in the trunk and leave it there for the next two days. And we will have to find out the cost of the vase so that you can pay for it. I just want you to know that I love you, and that's why I take responsibility to help you learn to follow the rules." The most effective way to teach a child obedience is to wrap discipline in love. Even when suffering the consequences, the child is assured of the parent's love. When a child feels loved, he is likely to receive the discipline as a fair consequence of his behavior.

Compare this to the common response of the parent who hears the vase fall from the mantel, dashes to the living room, sees the child picking up the football, and yells, "I have told you a thousand times, don't throw the football in the living room! Now look at what you've done. That vase was bought by your grandmother; it's thirty years old. It's priceless, and you destroyed it. When are you ever going to learn? You act like a two-year-old. I don't know what I'm going to do with you. Get out of here!" And the parent slaps him on the bottom as he leaves the room.

Which of these two approaches is more likely to teach the child healthy obedience? I think most parents will agree that the plan of clarifying the rule, agreeing upon the consequences of misbehavior before it happens, and lovingly but firmly applying the consequences to the child is far more productive both for the child's learning and the parents' mental health.

CHILDREN NEED TO LEARN
TO MAKE WISE DECISIONS

A third foundation in child rearing is teaching children to make wise decisions. In adulthood, success or failure in life is largely dependent upon the ability to make wise decisions.

How do children learn to make decisions? The process begins by giving them the freedom to make decisions within boundaries. You might say to your four-year-old daughter, "Do you want to bring your tricycle inside before dinner or after dinner?" The child has a choice. Either decision is within the boundaries of her parent's desires. If, however, she chooses to wait until after dinner and then forgets entirely to bring in the tricycle, she must suffer the consequences of having the tricycle impounded for two days. And if it rains during the night, she must wipe the rain off the tricycle. In this process, she probably learns it is better to bring the tricycle in before dinner while she is thinking about it, lest she forget later.

Or take the matter of eating lunch. If a child's response to the lunch you have prepared is "Yuck! I don't like this. I'm not going to eat it," then a wise parent gives the child the freedom to make that decision. "That's fine, honey. Why don't you run along and play?" However, if later in the afternoon the child comes asking for a snack because "I'm hungry, Mommy," the mother's response should be, "I bet you are, honey. It's probably because you didn't eat your lunch. Run along and play. We will have dinner later." The child made a decision, and the child suffered the consequences. He or she will probably think twice before refusing lunch again.

Then there is the bedtime ritual. Let's say that the bedtime routine is a drink of water or milk, a bedtime story, a prayer, kisses and hugs, and being tucked in by a parent. The rule is that if the child gets out of bed after having been tucked in there is no second drink of water, no second story, no second prayer, and no second tuck in. The child must get back into bed alone and settle in. Thus, the child has the freedom to make a decision—stay in bed the first time or no tuck in the second time. Most children will learn quickly that the parental tuck in is always the better of the two choices.

Sometimes small children will throw temper tantrums in order to get parents to change the rules. If a child's temper tantrum is accompanied with demands to be taken to the parents' room or to get another drink of water, a parent can simply state, "If you want to continue yelling and screaming, you can do it for two more minutes. But if you go beyond two minutes, it means tomorrow night you will go to bed fifteen minutes earlier than your bedtime." Once children learn that all behavior has consequences, they quickly learn to change their behavior.

If a child throws a temper tantrum in the middle of the day, the parent can simply remind the child, "We don't get things by throwing temper tantrums. In fact, if you wish to continue screaming and crying, then I will put you in your room where you can do that; but you are not going to do it in my presence." Thus, the child has the freedom to throw a temper tantrum, but he or she must do it in isolation, not in your presence. Temper tantrums quickly subside when children realize that they are not acceptable behavior and they do not get the desired outcome.

As children get older, they should be assigned household responsibilities that aid in the function of the family. For example, a four-year-old can put his or her soiled clothes in the laundry hamper. As time goes on, household responsibilities expand with their expanding abilities. Once a chore is assigned and a time designated by which the chore is to be completed, a child has the choice to complete the chore or not to complete the chore. If the chore is not completed by the appointed time, then some other family member has an opportunity to do the chore and be paid out of the child's allowance. Thus, the child has a choice to do the chore on time or not to do the chore, but he or she also suffers the consequence if the chore is not done. Children learn quickly when they are held accountable for their own behavior.

What about fighting in the backseat of the car? Many parents get extremely frustrated in their efforts to stop children from fighting. My suggestion is that you give them the freedom to fight, but not in the backseat of the car. As soon as they start fighting, you remind them of the rule: no fighting in the car. They also know the consequences: If they continue to fight, you will pull the car to the side of the road. The two of them will get outside to continue their fighting. When they finish, they may get back into the car. If the family is on the way to get ice-cream cones, you can imagine how quickly the fighting will subside. The parents are not frustrated, and the children have learned a valuable lesson: We have choices, but if we make poor choices, we have to suffer the consequences.

The same principle applies in teaching children good manners. For example, if you have a rule that when someone gives your son a gift he says thank you, and the consequence of not saying it is that he doesn't get to play with the gift until he says it, the child learns to say thank you. Or, if you are at Grandmother's house and Grandmother gives him a gift, you don't prod him, you simply wait to see what he does. If he forgets to say thank you, when you get home, you take the toy, put it in your closet, and tell him he can't play with it until he writes Grandmother a thank-you note. Children quickly learn that it pays to have good manners. If children leave the table without saying, "May I be excused, please?" they are required to come back to the table and sit while the parents wash the dishes. We are teaching children that life is composed of choices. When we make good choices, everybody is happier. When we make bad choices, the results are not pleasant.

It is this process of making choices between two alternatives that helps children learn the value of making wise decisions. You are doing them a great service, and you are removing a great deal of frustration from yourself. Forcing children to say thank you is simply getting compliance. But when they suffer the consequence of not saying thank you, they learn to say it.

When you give a child the opportunity to make decisions within boundaries, you are respecting the

dignity of the child. You are recognizing that the child is a person, not a machine. People have choices, and those choices always impact themselves and others. It is a valuable lesson for a child to learn.

One of the most common mistakes that parents make is threatening their children: "If you do that again . . ." Sometimes parents follow through with their threats if the bad behavior occurs again. Sometimes the parents do not. In my opinion, parents should never make threats; they should take loving action. Threats confuse a child; consistent action gives the child security. If a child violates a rule, the parents should administer the consequences immediately with calmness and love. An added bonus is that when a parent replaces threats with action, the parent is less likely to grow frustrated and, in the heat of anger, overreact.

There is no place for a parent to lose his or her temper with a child. Beating or yelling and screaming at a child are always negative. Calmly administering the consequences of negative behavior is the most effective way to teach children how to make wise decisions.

The pattern of discipline laid out in this chapter has helped thousands of parents learn how to effectively train their children. When a husband and wife feel that they are working together in training their children, it creates a more positive climate between them. You are working together in rearing these children, and you are consistent in applying the rules. You feel good about yourselves, and you feel good about your children. This atmosphere greatly enhances the marital relationship. If the two of you discuss and agree on the approach of child discipline as discussed in this chapter, I believe it will take you to a whole new level of effective discipline and create a much more positive climate for your marriage.

PUTTING THE PRINCIPLES INTO PRACTICE

1. If you do not know the primary love language of each of your children, let me encourage you to answer the following questions:

   - Which of the five love languages does my child most often express to others: Words

of Affirmation, Acts of Service, Gifts, Quality Time, or Physical Touch?

- Which of these five does my child most often complain about?

- Which of these five does my child most often request?

The answers to these three questions will tell you your child's primary love language. If you and your spouse can agree to give heavy doses of the primary love language to your child while sprinkling in the other four, you can be assured your child will feel loved.

2. Make sure your child knows your rules and the consequences of breaking the rules.

- Make a list of the rules that you have for your child. Ask your spouse to do the same. (Or perhaps you can make the list together.)

- What would be the most logical consequence if your child broke one of these rules? Discuss it and agree on what the consequence will be.

- Inform your child of the rules, and make clear what will happen if the rule is broken.

- Consistently follow through by taking action when your child breaks a rule. (It doesn't matter who administers the discipline. It will be the same by both parents because you have agreed on it.)

3. Think about times in the past when you have tried to force your child to do something and it has erupted into a major battle. Now, think of a way you could have given the child a choice that would have alleviated the conflict and perhaps helped the child learn how to make wise decisions. Here are some examples to get you started: to eat or not to eat, to bring a toy in before dinner or after dinner, to complete the chores on time or not to complete the chores, to stay in bed or to get out of bed. Perhaps you can add to this list.

The more choices you allow your child to make, the more quickly your child will learn the difference between poor decisions and wise decisions, and the less conflict you will have.

5

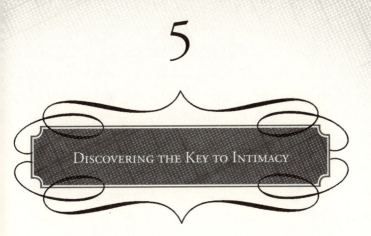

DISCOVERING THE KEY TO INTIMACY

$\mathscr{A}$t the heart of a healthy marriage is a deep sense of being connected, loved, appreciated, and respected—intimacy. We had it when we got married, or at least we thought we did. In the dating phase of our relationship, we spent hours talking. We respected each other's ideas. There was a sense of openness between the two of us. We felt as if we "belonged" to each other, that we were "meant" for each other. We shared our deepest secrets and believed in our hearts that we would love each other no matter what happened.

Do you remember the promises you made in those days? "Nothing you could ever tell me will cause me to stop loving you." "I'll go anywhere with you." "Whatever is best for you is what I want as long as I live." It was the belief that you had an intimate relationship unlike anything you had ever experienced before that led you to the commitment of marriage.

Sadly enough, this taste of intimacy is far too brief for many couples. Sometimes it evaporates even before the children arrive. For other couples, it begins to erode upon the arrival of the first child. As one husband said, "I don't know what happened. I thought we were doing pretty well until the baby came. After that, it has been all downhill. Before the baby, she was loving, exciting, and caring. After the baby, she became demanding and critical." His wife's response? "Before the baby, he was thoughtful. I was the focus of his life. After the baby, it was as though I didn't matter anymore. I tried to lose weight quickly. I tried to get back in shape, but nothing seemed to help. Everything else was more important to him than I am." Both of them felt disconnected, unloved, and unappreciated.

Many couples echo the sentiments of this couple. They are badgered by the secret fear, "We should not have married. We don't really love each other." They long for what they thought they had when they got married—a deeply intimate, supportive relationship.

What many couples do not understand is that love must be nurtured. Intimacy is not static. You don't "get it" and have it forever. We move in and out of intimacy based on our behavior toward each other. Chances are you would not be reading this if you had the level of intimacy you desire in your marriage. You are probably among the thousands who wish their marriage could be better. I want to assure you that your dream can come true.

The arrival of children may well have diminished your marital intimacy, but the presence of children need not keep you from building an intimate marriage. We have talked about taking control of your schedule in order to make time for each other. We have also talked about taking control of your money so that you can afford the kinds of things that build intimacy. We have discussed ideas on child rearing that will lower the stress level. The only missing ingredient is discovering the key to intimacy. How do you build or rebuild intimacy in your relationship? What do you do with the time and money you have created? Time and money alone will not build intimacy; it's how you use your time and money. In this chapter, I want to give you three essential ingredients in building an intimate marriage while at the same time being good parents.

REMOVING THE RUBBLE

Perhaps you have seen houses that have been destroyed by fire, flood, or wind. Where a house once stood, there is rubble. The first step in rebuilding the house is to remove the rubble. The foundation will likely still exist, but you can't build on the foundation until you remove the rubble.

If in your marriage the dry winds have blown and the floods have come and the level of intimacy in your marriage is less than in previous years, it is extremely likely that the foundation is still there. It's time to remove the rubble.

So how do you remove the rubble? You begin by acknowledging that you are a part of the problem. Typically, we can see the failures of our spouse much more clearly than we can see our own failures. If you are going to remove the rubble, you must begin by identifying and acknowledging your part in the demolition of your intimacy. Three elements typically destroy intimacy: The first element is harsh, critical, condemning words. The second is hurtful actions. And the third is neglect. These three destroy our sense of being connected, loved, appreciated, and respected. Perhaps you would be willing to invest a few moments with God and ask him to show you the role your unkind words, hurtful actions, and neglect have played in destroying the intimacy of your marriage. If you are willing to ask God, God is willing to answer.

Another part of the rubble-removal process is confessing your failures to your spouse and asking for forgiveness. Would you be willing to say something like this to your spouse? "I know that my actions have hurt you deeply. My words have been unkind and unfair. I have neglected you. And in so doing, I have diminished what I want most in life—an intimate relationship with you. I cannot undo what I have done, but if you will forgive me, I would like to show you that I do indeed love you, respect you, and appreciate you. I know that we both have many stresses on us with the children, our jobs, and our other responsibilities. But I believe that together we can build a healthy marriage, and that is what I want." When you do this, you have taken the first step in rebuilding intimacy in your marriage.

Let me warn you that your spouse may not reciprocate quickly. He or she may not be ready to forgive you and may not admit to failing in the relationship. Don't expect too much. Rather, allow time to see that you are sincere, that you are not simply trying to brush the past away, and that you are genuinely seeking to build a new relationship.[1]

REAFFIRMING YOUR COMMITMENT

Perhaps you have forgotten the words, "I promise to love, honor, and keep you, in sickness and in health, in poverty and in wealth, so long as we both shall live." Perhaps on the day you married, you were so enamored by the euphoric feelings of being "in love" that you failed to reflect deeply on these words. They are heavy words, but they are the words to which you need to return if you want to renew an intimate relationship. True love is not a feeling. It is an attitude—a choice made daily to look out for the well-being of your spouse, to find ways to enhance and enrich his or her life. It is the choice to invest time, energy, and money to accomplish that goal. Bottom line—love is the commitment to be there for each other *no matter what.*

The Bible challenges the husband to love his wife as Christ "loved the church and gave himself up for her."[2] Let me remind you that Christ loved the church before the church loved him. He loved the church even when the church was rejecting his love. And he loved the church all the way to death.

The wife is challenged to "respect her husband"[3] and to allow him the privilege of loving her. Some women find this difficult because they have been reared in a culture that teaches them to be assertive and take care of themselves. However, it is the willingness to admit that spouses need each other that leads to marital intimacy. We were not made to live in isolation. We were meant to live deeply connected to each other, each of us looking out for the interests of the other and working together as a team to become the people God intended us to be. That is what marriage is all about. And the best parents are those who have this kind of marriage.

If you are willing to reaffirm your commitment, perhaps you could contact the person who performed your wedding ceremony and ask if he has a copy of the vows you made to each other. If this is not possible, I have included at the end of this book the vows from a typical wedding ceremony. Perhaps they are close enough to the ones you made that you would be willing to verbally affirm them to your spouse. Again, let me warn you that your spouse may or may not be willing to reciprocate. The pain may be too deep, and hope may have evaporated. Emotionally, perhaps your spouse is not presently able to affirm these vows to you. Don't expect it, and don't demand it. Give your spouse time, while you continue to demonstrate that you are serious about the changes that are taking place in your own life.

MAKING YOUR SPOUSE FEEL LOVED

Finding out what makes your spouse feel loved and appreciated—and then doing it consistently—may take a while. But you can do it. Let me give you some possible approaches.

Now that you have acknowledged to your spouse your failures of the past and you have verbally reaffirmed your commitment, you are ready to say, "As you know, I am trying to become the husband/wife that you deserve. So, what could I do to help you this evening?" Whatever your spouse suggests, you not only do it to the best of your ability but you write it down in a notebook. For example:

- She likes it when I fold the towels.

- He likes it when I give him a back rub.

You ask your question every night: "What could I do to help you this evening?" And every evening, you do it and write it down, if it is not already on your list. On the simplest and easiest level, you are learning how to love and express appreciation to your spouse.

As time goes on, you ask similar questions in different social settings. For example, as you drive to church you might say, "We've been going to church a long time, but I would like to ask you, 'What could I do differently at church that would make things more meaningful for you?'" Do it, and write it in your notebook:

- She likes it when I let her talk with friends after church instead of pulling on her arm, telling her it is time to go home.

- He likes it when I sit beside him in church rather than singing in the choir.

The willingness to give, the willingness to sacrifice— this is true love, and it builds marital intimacy.

As the atmosphere between the two of you begins to improve, you might ask this question:

"What could I do that would make me a better husband [or wife] to you?" With this question, you are broadening the scope for suggestions. You may address any area of life. Whatever your spouse shares you can take seriously and know that he or she is giving you valuable information on how to express love and appreciation. Do it and record it. And you will be on the road to greater intimacy.

However, not all spouses will respond positively to this approach. You may say, "What could I do to help you this evening?" and your spouse may respond, "If I have to tell you, then it doesn't mean anything to me." Or perhaps the response is "I don't want you to help me. Just stay out of my way." Either of these or similar responses indicate that your spouse has been deeply hurt and is emotionally fatigued from the lack of intimacy in the relationship. Your spouse is not highly motivated to give you an opportunity to try because there is little hope that you will be consistent.

The fact that your spouse has lost hope does not mean that you must also abandon hope. There is another approach to discovering what makes your spouse feel loved and appreciated. It's called *evaluating the criticisms.*

Look back over the years and ask yourself, "What has my spouse complained about through the years? What has my spouse nagged me about?" Perhaps at the time, you resented the criticisms and rebelled at the nagging. In fact, you were getting valuable information. Your spouse was telling you what made him or her feel loved and appreciated. This approach opens up a whole new vista of understanding your spouse.

I remember the husband who said to me after he tried this approach, "It all became so clear. In the earlier years, she nagged me about taking the trash outside every night after dinner. I wanted to wait until the trash bag was full. Finally, she started taking it out herself. Now I realize that I had blown an opportunity to express love to her. So without saying a word, I started taking the trash out every night after dinner.

"I remembered also that she used to complain that I didn't vacuum her car every time I vacuumed my truck. Personally, I didn't think her car needed it as often as my truck. Now I realize that to her that would have been an expression of love. So without saying a word, I started washing and vacuuming her car every time I washed and vacuumed my truck. I remembered a few more criticisms, and I started doing the things she had requested. After about three months, she said to me, 'What's going on with you?' I simply said, 'Remember when I told you that I was sorry for my past failures? And I told you I was committed to becoming the husband you deserve? Well, I've just been working at it. I know you deserve a whole lot more than I've given you through the years, and I intend to give it to you from this point on.' She walked away without giving me any verbal response, but within a month, one day she smiled and said to me, 'I can't believe the things you have been doing for me. I'm beginning to enjoy living with you again. You are becoming the man I married. I just hope I don't wake up and find out I was dreaming.'

"From that day, the atmosphere in our marriage has been radically different. From that point

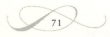

GARY CHAPMAN

on, she would answer my question when I asked, 'What can I do to help you this evening?' She made suggestions and I did them. Before long, she started asking me what she could do to make my life better. That was the day I started having romantic feelings for her again. Once the atmosphere got better, we started talking again, looking back over the past and discussing where we both went wrong. We've learned a lot about each other. I never knew that my taking the trash out consistently made her more interested in having sex. I wish someone had told me that twenty years ago. Even the kids have noticed the difference in our marriage. Our twelve-year-old son recently said to us, 'I don't know what's going on with you two. But I want you to know I like it. I was tired of the yelling and screaming. I'm glad to see that you two are finally getting it together.' He went on to tell us how hard it was to live in the house with us when we were not getting along. Neither of us realized that our behavior had so deeply impacted him. We took the occasion to apologize to him and asked his forgiveness for our failures. I'm just glad that we are finally learning how to love each other."

In the early years of marriage, most couples are expressing love to each other. The problem is that often they are not expressing love in a way the other person understands. Typically we are doing for each other what our parents did for each other, or we are doing for them what we wish they would do for us. One young man told me that for the first six months of his marriage, every month he would bring his wife a dozen roses on the date of their anniversary. He did this because that's what his father did for his mother. It took her six months to get up the courage to tell him that she didn't particularly care for roses, and in fact, she was somewhat allergic to them. He was disillusioned to find out that what was meaningful to his mother was not so meaningful to his wife. One young wife served her husband breakfast in bed every Saturday morning for the first month of their marriage because that's what her mother did. She later discovered that he much preferred eating at the table.

Sincerity is not enough. We must ask questions if we are to discover what is meaningful to the other person. What makes one person feel loved does not necessarily make another person feel loved. That is why a husband and wife can be genuinely express-ing love to each other, and yet neither feels loved or appreciated. When you express love in a way that is meaningful to your spouse, you are build-ing intimacy.

As the emotional climate between the two of you is built up, you may periodically want to ask your spouse, "What could we do to improve our marriage?" If you discover that a weekend getaway is meaningful to your spouse, then put it on your schedule and find the money to do it. If you dis-cover that a weekly date night makes her feel con-nected to you, then by all means hire a babysitter or trade off with another couple who has children approximately the age of your children, and make it happen. If you discover that a "sit down and talk" time each evening is what makes your spouse feel loved and appreciated, then put it into your daily schedule and make it as important as reporting to work in the morning.

It's the simple things, sometimes little things, that make or break a marriage. The wise couple will discover what makes the other feel connected, loved, appreciated, and respected. And they will do it. Intimacy flourishes, and the children have the benefit of growing up in a home where Mom and Dad love and support each other. What greater gift could you give any child?

PUTTING THE PRINCIPLES INTO PRACTICE

1. Removing the Rubble: If you have not already done so, why not take a few minutes to think about how you contributed to the lack of intimacy in your marriage? Ask God to remind you of harsh, critical, condemning words; hurtful actions; and times of neglect. Once you have confessed these to God, why not acknowledge them to your spouse and ask forgiveness?

2. Reaffirming Your Commitment: Would you be willing to contact the person who performed your wedding ceremony and ask if he could send you a copy of the vows you made when you were married? If this is not

possible, utilize the vows at the end of this book. Affirm those vows to God and then to your spouse.

3. Making Your Spouse Feel Loved: Using one of the two methods in this chapter, discover the things that make your spouse feel loved and appreciated. The first approach is to ask questions: "What could I do to help you this evening?" "How could I be a better husband/wife to you?" "What could I do at church or at the mall to make the experience more meaningful for you?" The second approach is to examine the criticisms of the past to discover what is meaningful to your spouse. What your spouse has complained about reveals his or her inner desires.

In a notebook, list the things that you know are meaningful to your spouse and seek to express love in these ways on a regular basis.

*W*hat I have shared with you in the brief pages of this book has helped hundreds of couples discover how to have a successful marriage and at the same time be successful parents. God never intended children to destroy marriages. On the other hand, neither do children create strong marriages. Strong marriages are created by husbands and wives who put their hands in the hand of the God who created marriage and ordained that children would flourish best in a home with a mom and dad who love, support, and encourage each other.

Many couples complain that they don't have

the time or money to enrich their marriages. I believe that such complaints are ill-spoken. You have the time and you have the money to do everything you ought to do for each other and for your children. You may not yet have taken control of your schedules or taken control of your money, but you have the ability to do so. In this book, I have tried to give practical suggestions that will help you do both. If you apply these ideas, you will be able to create the time and the financial means to enrich your marriage—to keep intimacy alive while raising your children. To do so is one of the greatest things you can do for each other and for your children. I challenge you to implement the plan laid out in this book. I assure you that it works.

If you find this book helpful, I hope you will share it with a friend. If you have stories to share with me, I invite you to select the Contact link at www.garychapman.org.

Some Thoughts Worth Remembering

- If an intimate marriage and parenting are both a part of God's design, then surely there is a way to do both successfully.

- What does it mean to make marriage a priority? It means, first, that we pause long enough to assess the quality of our marriage. Then we must make a conscious choice that for the benefit of our children, for ourselves, and (if we are Christians) for the glory of God, we will commit ourselves to each other and acknowledge that our marriage is important to us.

Finally, we must agree that with God's help we will find a way to strengthen our intimacy.

🖝 I believe that the answer to finding time to build a strong marriage, while at the same time being good parents, lies in taking control of our schedules.

🖝 Getting control of your schedule means getting the right person doing the right task and deciding when it will be done, eliminating any unnecessary tasks that you are presently doing, getting your children on a schedule that interfaces positively with your schedule, and making time for yourself.

🖝 There is a simple principle that, when applied, will keep a marriage alive regardless of a couple's income. The principle is this: Put your money where your priorities are.

🖝 The best things in life are free—or at least inexpensive. Taking time to enjoy a sunset, picking a wildflower and giving it to your spouse, enjoying the colors of fall leaves, going to church, taking a walk together, or sitting together on the porch while the crickets serenade you costs nothing! Sharing ice-cream cones, eating your favorite pizza, and taking a swim or attending a movie together are all relatively inexpensive.

~ The word *discipline* is not a negative word, nor is it to be equated with spanking or yelling at children. The word *discipline* means literally "to train." Most parents recognize that children need training. Without positive discipline, children will self-destruct; they cannot train themselves.

~ In adulthood, success or failure in life is largely dependent upon the ability to make wise decisions. How do children learn to make decisions? The process begins by giving them the freedom to make decisions within boundaries.

When a husband and wife feel that they are working together in training their children, it creates a more positive climate between them. You are working together to rear these children, and you are consistent in applying the rules. You feel good about yourselves, and you feel good about your children. This atmosphere greatly enhances the marital relationship.

The Bible challenges the husband to love his wife as Christ "loved the church and gave himself up for her" (Ephesians 5:25). Christ loved the church before the church loved him. He loved the church even when the church was rejecting his love. And he loved the church all the way to death.

The wife is challenged to "respect her husband" (Ephesians 5:33) and to allow him the privilege of loving her. Some women find this difficult when they have been reared in a culture that teaches them to be assertive and take care of themselves. However, it is the willingness to admit that spouses need each other that leads to marital intimacy.

🖙 Finding out what makes your spouse feel loved and appreciated—and then doing it consistently—may take a while. But you can do it.

🖙 Look back over the years and ask yourself, "What has my spouse complained about through the years? What has my spouse nagged me about?" Perhaps at the time you resented the criticisms and rebelled at the nagging. In fact, you were getting valuable information. Your spouse was telling you what made him or her feel loved and appreciated.

🖙 What makes one person feel loved does not necessarily make another person feel loved. That is why a husband and wife can be genuinely expressing love to each other, and yet neither feels loved or appreciated. When you express love in a way that is meaningful to your spouse, you are building intimacy.

⌐ *Traditional Wedding Vows*

THE HUSBAND SPEAKING:

*I, _____, take thee, _____, to be my wedded wife . . .
to have and to hold from this day forward . . . for better, for worse,
for richer, for poorer . . . in sickness and in health. To love and to
cherish . . . so long as we both shall live, according to God's holy
ordinance, and hereto I pledge thee my faithfulness.*

THE WIFE SPEAKING:

*I, _____, take thee, _____, to be my wedded
husband . . . to have and to hold from this day forward . . . for
better, for worse, for richer, for poorer . . . in sickness and in health.
To love and to cherish . . . so long as we both shall live, according
to God's holy ordinance, and hereto I pledge thee my faithfulness.*

⌒ *Notes*

INTRODUCTION
1. Carolyn Pape Cowan and Philip A. Cowan, *When Partners Become Parents* (HarperCollins, 1992), 109.
2. Ibid., 89.

CHAPTER 1
1. Genesis 1:28.
2. Genesis 2:24.
3. Alice Gray, comp., *Stories for a Mom's Heart* (Sisters, Ore.: Multnomah, 2002), 29.
4. Jimmy Van Heusen and Sammy Cahn, "Love and Marriage," copyright 1955 by Barton Music Corp./Warner Chappell Music, Inc.
5. For more information on the four seasons concept, you may wish to read *The Four Seasons of Marriage,* by Gary Chapman (Carol Stream, Ill.: Tyndale House, 2005).

CHAPTER 3
1. *MSN Money* staff, "Raising Your Quarter-Million-Dollar Baby," located at http://moneycentral.msn.com/content/ collegeandfamily/raisekids/p37245.asp.

CHAPTER 4
1. For more information on the love-languages concept, you may wish to read *The Five Love Languages of Children,* written by Gary Chapman and Ross Campbell (Chicago: Northfield Publishing, 1997).

CHAPTER 5

1. For further help in how to apologize successfully, you may wish to read *The Five Languages of Apology*, by Gary Chapman and Jennifer Thomas (Chicago: Northfield Publishing, 2006).
2. Ephesians 5:25.
3. Ephesians 5:33.

About the Author

Dr. Gary Chapman is the author of the perennial best seller *The Five Love Languages* (more than 3.5 million copies sold) and numerous other marriage and family books. He is currently working with best-selling author Catherine Palmer on a new fiction series based on *The Four Seasons of Marriage*, the first book of which was released in the spring of 2007. Dr. Chapman is the director of Marriage and Family Life Consultants, Inc.; an internationally known speaker; and the host of *A Growing Marriage*, a syndicated radio program heard on more than one hundred stations across North America. He and his wife, Karolyn, live in North Carolina.

DO YOU KNOW WHICH SEASON
YOUR MARRIAGE IS IN?

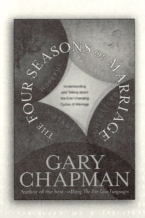

Every marriage goes through different seasons—
the satisfaction and security of summer, the
hopefulness and anticipation of spring, the
change and uncertainty of fall, and the icy
bitterness of winter. Find out which season your
marriage is currently in and learn the strategies
that will strengthen your relationship through
every season of marriage.

Available now in stores and online!

Take the free marriage-satisfaction quiz at
www.4seasonsofmarriage.com